BRIGHT NOTES

KON-TIKI AND AKU-AKU BY THOR HEYERDAHL

Intelligent Education

Nashville, Tennessee

BRIGHT NOTES: Kon-Tiki and Aku-Aku
www.BrightNotes.com

No part of this publication may be used or reproduced in any manner whatsoever without written permission, except in the case of brief quotations in critical articles and reviews. For permissions, contact Influence Publishers http://www.influencepublishers.com.

ISBN: 978-1-645425-04-5 (Paperback)
ISBN: 978-1-645425-05-2 (eBook)

Published in accordance with the U.S. Copyright Office Orphan Works and Mass Digitization report of the register of copyrights, June 2015.

Originally published by Monarch Press.
Thomas A. Duff, 1966
2020 Edition published by Influence Publishers.

Interior design by Lapiz Digital Services. Cover Design by Thinkpen Designs.

Printed in the United States of America.

Library of Congress Cataloging-in-Publication Data forthcoming.
Names: Intelligent Education
Title: BRIGHT NOTES: Kon-Tiki and Aku-Aku
Subject: STU004000 STUDY AIDS / Book Notes

CONTENTS

1) Introduction To Thor Heyerdahl — 1

2) Kon-Tiki Textual Analysis — 6
    Chapter One: A Theory — 6
    Chapter Two: An Expedition Is Born — 9
    Chapter Three: To South America — 11
    Chapter Four: Across The Pacific — 13
    Chapter Five: Halfway — 15
    Chapter Six: Across The Pacific — 17
    Chapter Seven: To The South Sea Islands — 19
    Chapter Eight: Among Polynesians — 21

3) Aku-Aku Textual Analysis — 23
    Chapter One: Detectives Off To The End Of The World — 23
    Chapter Two: What Awaited Us At The World's Navel — 25
    Chapter Three: In Volcanic Gas Tunnels — 27
    Chapter Four: The Mystery Of The Easter Island Giants — 29
    Chapter Five: The Long Ears' Secret — 31
    Chapter Six: Superstition Against Superstition — 33
    Chapter Seven: Meeting The Caves' Dumb Guardians — 36
    Chapter Eight: Into The Secret Caves — 38
    Chapter Nine: Among Gods And Devils — 40

	Chapter Ten: A Ruined City In The Clouds	42
	Chapter Eleven: My Aku-Aku Says	44
4)	Critical Commentary	46
5)	Essay Questions and Answers	50
6)	Bibliography	55

INTRODUCTION TO THOR HEYERDAHL

Thor Heyerdahl was born in Larvik, Norway, on October 6, 1914. His father was the president of a brewery and mineral water plant; his mother was Alison (nee Lyng) Heyerdahl, the chairlady of the Larvik Museum. Heyerdahl's choice of a career was influenced by the interests of his parents: his father loved outdoor life - hiking, hunting, and fishing - and his mother loved zoology, folk art, and the study of primitive races. The young boy decided to become a zoologist; he studied at the Middelskole of Larvik, graduating when he was sixteen. Three years later he graduated from the Larvik Gymnasium and enrolled at Oslo University. At the University, he studied mathematics, philosophy, genetics, zoology, and geography. In addition, he specialized in the study of Polynesian ethnology. During his school vacations, Heyerdahl sought a change from his academic pursuits by fishing in mountain lakes and streams, camping out in the mountain forests, and hiking over snow-covered trails in dog-sleds pulled by teams of barking huskies. His desire to write about his experiences found expression in the articles he began to publish in Norwegian newspapers and magazines.

In December, 1936, Heyerdahl decided to leave his studies at the University to embark on a zoological-ethnological expedition to the Marquesas Islands in French Oceania in the South Pacific. Both he and his wife, Liv Heyerdahl, whom he had married on

Christmas Eve of 1936, had shared the hope of "getting back to nature" by traveling to a primitive region far from the stresses and strains of modern life. The Museum of the University of Oslo had agreed to cooperate with Heyerdahl in the planning of the expedition, although he paid for the expenses of the trip himself, inasmuch as he would be able to use the trip as the practical field experience needed for him to obtain his advanced degree at the university.

After a successful voyage, Heyerdahl and his wife landed at Fatu-Hiva, the exotic Marquesan island which was to become their home for the next two years. Living as the natives did, on simple fruits, fish, and coconuts, the Heyerdahls had found the tranquility which they had sought. But they were also very busy. Heyerdahl explored native trails, navigated the sinuous rivers and streams, and made a remarkable discovery: the ruins of ancient temples with carvings in red stone of grotesque figures chiseled centuries ago. His findings were to change Heyerdahl's primary interest from zoology to ethnology, and were the basis for his later research and travel, particularly for his Kon-Tiki voyage and the later exploration of Easter Island, recounted in *Aku-Aku*. Heyerdahl compiled a Norwegian - Polynesian dictionary through his study of the natives' language on Fatu-Hiva, and published an article on his experiences of 1937-38 in the January, 1941, issue of the *National Geographic Magazine*.

Why was Heyerdahl fascinated with the early art of the Marquesan Islands? Primarily, because he thought these relics bore a marked resemblance to artistic works of early tribes of South America. Many of the legends he had heard from the natives of Fatu-Hiva were similar to those tales of South America native to the Indian tribes who lived before the Incas. Was there any connection between the two cultures? If so, how could one tribe have possibly influenced the other, unless it were possible for the natives of centuries ago to have crossed the Pacific Ocean? This question was the one that Heyerdahl would, someday perhaps, try to answer.

Heyerdahl returned to Norway in 1938, and published *Paa Jakt efter Paradiset* (*On the Hunt for Paradise*). He spent the next year in library research in Oslo, and then did research among the coastal Indians in Bella Paula, British Columbia (1939-1940). He spent 1940-1942 working at various jobs in Canada and the United States. During World War II, he served in the Norwegian armed forces as a lieutenant, first in a parachute unit and later in an invasion unit which operated in Arctic Norway until the end of the war.

After the war, Heyerdahl returned to his studies of Polynesian culture. His chief theory was that the prehistoric settlement of the South Seas Islands was made by ancient pre-Inca Indians from Peru, who had worshipped the sun god "Kon." The leader of this race, he believed, was Kon-Tiki, "the earthly representative of Kon," who fled about A.D. 500 with some of his followers across the Pacific after a war with Indians from the Andes mountains. Heyerdahl was determined to prove that the pre-historic Peruvians could have sailed across the ocean on their balsa-wood rafts by means of strong ocean currents. With five of his companions, he set sail on a wooden craft, the Kon-Tiki, from Callao, Peru, on April 28, 1947. His five companions were Herman Watzinger, Knut Haugland, Bengt Danielsson, Erik Hesselberg, and Torstein Raaby. Their "other" purposes were to collect oceanographic data and to "test life-saving and communications equipment developed by the United States and British armed forces during and since the war."

After a trip of one hundred and one days, the raft reached the Tuamotu Archipelago, where it was wrecked on the Raroia

Reef. But the voyage had been a success. President Truman of the United States and King Haakon of Norway, among others, saluted Heyerdahl and his companions for their historic voyage. A best-selling book, *Kon-Tiki*, and a prize-winning documentary film of the trip made Heyerdahl famous throughout the world.

Heyerdahl did not take his wife on the Kon-Tiki voyage, explaining: "My wife wanted to go along on this trip, because she's just as sure I'm right about this idea, and just as adventure-minded as I am, but we decided that one of us had better stay at home and look after our adventurous kids." His family, including a son and daughter, did accompany him, however, on a later voyage to Easter Islands. A large modern ship provided the kind of living accommodations less readily available on a wooden raft. In his later book, *Aku-Aku*, Heyerdahl tells how his curiosity about Easter Island first became whetted: "As the Kon-Tiki drifted with the current far to the north, we had sat on deck in the moonlight and talked about the mystery of Easter Island. At that time I had secretly dreamed of coming back some-day to the eastern Pacific and going ashore to the lovely island." Excavations made at Easter Island have produced numerous artifacts of a civilization which may have flourished before the birth of Christ. The book is a recounting of the adventures Heyerdahl and his group encountered, and ends with his speculation on the origins and past history of the island. (See Critical Commentary.)

Heyerdahl still continues to make his great interest in outdoor life and traveling part of his yearly routine. In addition to his writing, he has also cultivated less active hobbies in woodcarving and cartooning. The energy, devotion, and skill with which Heyerdahl has pursued knowledge of man and his world are attested to by a staggering list of medals, memberships in renowned societies, and other honors.

A partial listing of Thor Heyerdahl's citations include: Retzius Medal - Swedish Society for Anthropology and Geography, 1950; Mungo Park Medal - Royal Scottish Geographical Society, 1951; Prix Bonaparte-Wyse - Societe de Geographie, Paris, 1951; Elish Kent Kane Gold Medal - Geographic Society of Philadelphia, 1952; Vega Medal - Swedish Society of Anthropology and Geography, 1962; Lomonosov Medal - Moscow University, 1962; Oscar prize for best documentary - *Academy of Motion Pictures and Sciences*, 1952; and Member of Royal Norwegian Academy of Arts and Sciences.

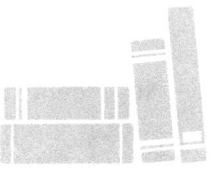

KON-TIKI

TEXTUAL ANALYSIS

CHAPTER ONE: A THEORY

In this opening chapter the author, Thor Heyerdahl, endeavors to explain how, on May 17, 1947, Norwegian Independence Day, he came to find himself at sea on a wooden raft with a parrot and five companions, eight hundred and fifty sea miles from the coast of Peru. The adventure might have begun the winter before, in the office of a New York museum, or even ten years earlier on Fatu Hiva, one of the Marquesas Islands in the middle of the Pacific. At that time, the author was accompanied by his wife in collecting all kinds of live creatures as well as relics of a past culture. One night, an old man told him the story of Kon-Tiki, the chief god, son of the sun, who had brought his ancestors to the island. Later the thought struck the author that the stone figures of Tiki found in the jungle had a remarkable similarity to the monoliths left by extinct South American civilizations.

Upon returning to Norway, Heyerdahl embarked upon intensive studies of the peoples who inhabited the islands of the eastern Pacific. He discovered that the question of where the original inhabitants of these islands came from had never been answered fully, although it was absolutely certain that the original Polynesian race had, at some time, come drifting or sailing to these islands. A study of local genealogies on the islands showed that the South Sea islands were not peopled before about A.D. 500. A still later migration reached the islands about A.D. 1100. Heyerdahl noted that these people were of a Stone Age culture, as relics on the islands demonstrated. The only other civilizations at a similar cultural level at that time were found in the New World, where the highest Indian civilizations were ignorant of the use of iron. Thus Heyerdahl's attention was turned away from the Old World and over to the Indian civilizations of America.

On the nearest coast due east, in Peru, Heyerdahl felt there were traces of the origins of the Polynesians. An unknown people had once lived here and built a very strange civilization until they had vanished as though swept from the earth's surface. These peoples left behind them enormous stone statues in human forms similar to those on the Marquesas, Pitcairn, and Easter Islands, and pyramids like those found on Tahiti and Samoa. The Inca Indians told the first Spaniards who came to Peru of an earlier race of men with white skins and long beards who had come from the north and built these monuments. The Incas said they left as suddenly as they had come, fleeing westward across the Pacific. Heyerdahl notes that the first European to visit Polynesia discovered that many of the natives were of white complexion and bearded. Reading about the Inca legends of the sun-king Virakocha, head of the white people in Peru, he learned that the original name of Virakocha was Kon-Tiki, meaning Sun-Tiki or Fire-Tiki. Kon-Tiki was a priest and king of the white men living near Lake Titacaca who were massacred by the Incas. Kon-Tiki and a few others escaped, made their way to the Pacific coast and finally disappeared across the ocean.

Heyerdahl was thus certain that the chief god Sun-Tiki, driven from Peru by the Incas, was identical with the chief god Tiki, son of the sun, hailed as founder of the Polynesian race. Heyerdahl also believed that a second wave of Stone Age people or West Indians came to Polynesia around A.D. 1100, and he was seeking traces of these people on the western coast of British Columbia when he was forced to return to Norway because of the war in 1940. Upon the return of peace he decided to go to America to advance his theory.

Comment:

What an imaginative and exciting plan to sail four thousand miles across the Pacific Ocean to find out if it were possible for men of an earlier age to have done it! In his first chapter, Thor Heyerdahl reveals to the reader his idea for a bold sea voyage, the product of an exceptionally observant mind. Heyerdahl, we can see, has a natural bent for history and adventure.

Note:

This true narrative begins in the first person; most of Heyerdahl's prose will employ the first person plural "we" since he will be describing the experiences which he and his five comrades (Knut Haugland, Bengt Danielsson, Erik Hesselberg, Torstein Raaby, and Herman Watzinger) share in their remarkable raft voyage. For purposes of clarity, the summary of the incidents will be given in the present tense and in the third person.

KON-TIKI

TEXTUAL ANALYSIS

CHAPTER TWO: AN EXPEDITION IS BORN

....

It is now many years later and we find Heyerdahl in New York, on a trip to present his manuscript "Polynesia and America: A Study of Prehistoric Relations" to the director of a museum. At this time the author advances the idea that the original settlers of Polynesia crossed the ocean on balsa-wood rafts. When his theory is dismissed as "impossible" he determines to prove that it is possible to cross the Pacific by making a voyage himself on a raft. With the aid of a sailor friend he calculates that it will take exactly ninety-seven days to sail from Peru to the Tuamotu Islands. He seeks the advice of Peter Freuchen, who tells him he should go ahead with the expedition. When he decides to seek out five persons to accompany him on the raft, he chooses Knut Haugland, Bengt Danielsson, Erik Hesselberg, Torstein Raaby, and Herman Watzinger.

A problem which faces them is that of supply for the voyage. They do not wish to improvise their food supply on the basis of what the Indians had once taken on these voyages; they wished mainly to test the performance and quality of the Inca raft and whether the elements really would take it across the sea to Polynesia. A second desire was to find out whether, on the actual trip, they could obtain further supplies of fresh food and rain water while out at sea. They also required various forms of navigation equipment and day-to-day necessities. These problems are solved by the loan of certain articles for testing purposes from various sources. They also receive generous financial assistance sufficient to carry through the endeavor, so they can fly to South America and begin the building of the raft. Parenthetically, the author observes that the old Peruvian rafts were constructed of balsa wood, which is lighter than cork. Balsa wood is found in Peru, but since it grows in the Andes it was inaccessible to the Inca Indians along the sea coast, who therefore would have had to travel up the Pacific coast to Ecuador, where the balsa trees grow along the coast. The voyagers now intend to do the same. After having prepared the groundwork for their voyage, they leave for South America.

Comment:

Although we are reading a nonfiction work, there are many similarities between this diary-like account and a story. Our chief "character" is the narrator, Thor Heyerdahl, the man who relates the "plot" or-happenings aboard the raft "Kon-Tiki" and the "settings" - the humid, ebony jungles of South America, the lush green of the remote South Sea islands, and the majestic, chilling, and eternal ocean.

KON-TIKI

TEXTUAL ANALYSIS

CHAPTER THREE: TO SOUTH AMERICA

Once he arrives in Guayaquil, Ecuador, Heyerdahl sets out to find balsa logs suitable for a raft. Finding none along the seacoast, the group goes to Quito, high in the Andes, and from there to Quevedo, where there are large numbers of balsa trees to be found. Here they fell twelve long balsa trees. They name the logs in honor of legendary Polynesian figures whose origins can be traced to Peru. These logs are filled with sap and, since they weigh a ton apiece, there is a question of whether they will float on the water. They do float, however, as much above as below the surface of the water. The logs are then floated down the Palenque River and the Guayas River. They are then carried on a ship to Lima, where the task of fashioning them into a raft begins. Finally, they are ready to sail.

> Comment:

To a large extent, the raft which Heyerdahl and his friends built simulated the only kind of wooden structure which the natives of earlier cultures could possibly have made. Since the plan was to prove that men were able to cross the ocean some thousand years ago, it became imperative that modern men attempt the voyage under conditions closely approximating those of former times. Heyerdahl's raft, christened Kon-Tiki, first touched water on April 27, 1947. The next day it was towed by tugboat to western currents below the Equator.

KON-TIKI

TEXTUAL ANALYSIS

CHAPTER FOUR: ACROSS THE PACIFIC

On the afternoon of April 28, the raft Kon-Tiki is towed out of Callao harbor. The towing continues through the night at a slow speed. They are in the Humboldt Current, which brings warm water up the coast. Now one hundred miles from Lima, they continue on course. Days go by and the raft is tossed back and forth, to and fro. One cannot begin to see how high the waves fly. The water goes from blue to gray, and many weird-looking fish come from the sea. Steering is now a difficult problem. As the troughs of the sea grow deeper, it is clear that they have moved into the swiftest portion of the Humboldt Current - many times they wait uneasily to hear water smash down upon the raft. The sail thrashes against the bamboo cabin and threatens to destroy it. Another danger is that the raft may drift toward the Galapagos Islands, which are off course. On May 24, they are visited by a shark and they have sharks swimming alongside the raft for several days. Once they encounter a whale shark, the largest known and also the largest fish in the world today. This fish is exceedingly rare, but various specimens are found in the tropical oceans. It has an average length of fifty feet and weighs fifteen tons. The shark is finally chased off by harpoons. They are now in the South Equatorial Current, moving in a westerly direction four hundred sea miles south of the Galapagos. There is no longer, however, any danger of drifting into the Galapagos currents. They encounter large sea turtles which have come from these islands.

Comment:

As in any undertaking, the first step is usually the longest. We can imagine what an abrupt change in thinking takes place in a man's mind when he finds himself suddenly transported from the relatively secure soil of the land to the diminished square of a wooden raft, pitching and sloping over rugged ocean waves. The primary danger of ocean sailing is that a current may carry the powerless structure for hundreds of miles in a direction other than the one in which its sailors wish to go. In another famous work about a raft journey, Huckleberry Finn, Huck and his friend Jim have no real concern about the danger of unwanted currents since they are simply floating downstream on the Mississippi River.

There is, however, one great advantage that a small raft has above larger boats and ships - it maneuvers easily. The principle on which the Kon-Tiki succeeds is the same as that of a surf-board: the lightness and comparative balance of both crafts enable them to skim and ride the high waves, freeing them from the capsizing force which often strikes heavier, less agile craft.

KON-TIKI

TEXTUAL ANALYSIS

CHAPTER FIVE: HALFWAY

....

As the weeks pass, the crew of the Kon-Tiki see no sign of either a ship or of drifting remains to show that there are other people in the world. The whole sea is theirs. It is as though the salt in the air has cleansed both body and soul. Instead of being a fearsome enemy the elements have become reliable friends. The Indians with their leader, probably Kon-Tiki, had no serious food problems on their "original" voyage across the sea. In those days, the supplies consisted of what the natives took with them from land and what they obtained on the voyage. The Indians obtained water from rain on the sea. The food on the raft includes coconuts, tropical fruits, sweet potatoes, and plankton, tiny creatures of the deep.

Many kinds of sea creatures visit the raft. Whales come often. Most of the time their visitors are small porpoises and toothed whales. Various fish such as dolphins and pilot fish attach themselves to the raft. There are small black ants in some of the logs, and, when the raft has been at sea for a while, the dampness begins to penetrate the wood and the ants swarm out. Barnacles also are found on the sides of the raft. One of the members of the crew has the idea of building a diving basket by which they are able to look into the depths of the sea. They also are able to work out an ingenious system of steering by centerboards. At the halfway stage of the voyage they are about two thousand sea miles from the coast of South America, and it is the same distance to Polynesia in the west. The nearest land in any direction is the Galapagos Islands to east-northeast and Easter Island due south, both more than five hundred sea miles away. But they do not really feel these great distances, since the horizon glides along unnoticed as they move, and their own floating world is always the same.

Comment:

The crude basket used by the Kon-Tiki adventurers to explore, even briefly, the ocean depths emphasizes how curious man is about the world in which he lives. After planting flags in the North and South poles of the world, man has now turned his eyes to the skies, hungering after the moon and Mars. Similarly he has begun to dive below the surface of the sea, to record its treasures with increasingly more refined scientific instruments. Fascination with the lower depths, and his great curiosity, have led men to invent ingenious exploratory submarining laboratories, one of which, a remarkable inflatable rubber house (See Edward A. Link, "Out-post Under the Ocean," *National Geographic Magazine*, April, 1965), is designed to carry man to 442 feet below the surface of the sea, a depth unattainable to standard scuba gear.

KON-TIKI

TEXTUAL ANALYSIS

CHAPTER SIX: ACROSS THE PACIFIC

When the sea is not too rough some of the members of the expedition listen to the radio or go out in a dinghy (a small boat) to take pictures. When they see the silhouette of the craft grow smaller and smaller in the distance, a sensation of loneliness sometimes creeps over them. Still, going out in the dinghy is a diversion.

Comment:

Easter Island (Rapa Nui), one of the loneliest islands on the earth, fascinates Heyerdahl as they pass, and he muses on the Kon-Tiki deck about the possibility of someday landing there to explore. His reverie, however, became a reality and he recorded his impressions of Easter Island in *Aku-Aku*, which is summarized later in this review book.

The Kon-Tiki's short-wave radio is admittedly a modern device which gives the crew of the raft a lifeline with the world which the former voyagers could not enjoy. It must be reassuring to hear the music and commentary of "ham" operators from the various countries when one is surrounded by only water and sky. The element of safety should also be mentioned: in distress, a radio message could be readily dispatched, even though the hope of finding a raft in the ocean (without a fleet of helicopter patrols) is a slender one.

Heyerdahl reveals his knowledge of Polynesian weather habits by observing that a stationary cloud means land. In the southern Pacific islands, the tropical sun beats down on the land, baking it until streams of warmed air rise and are changed to cloud formations when they come in contact with colder levels of air.

KON-TIKI

TEXTUAL ANALYSIS

CHAPTER SEVEN: TO THE SOUTH SEA ISLANDS

On the night before July 30, the Kon-Tiki finally reaches sight of land. This proves to be the coral island of Puka-Puka, the first outpost of the Tuamotu group. They pass this island, however, because they are unable to buck the strong currents pulling them away from it. Four days later, they come in sight of the island of Angatau but are baffled in their efforts to come ashore by coral reefs surrounding the island. They spend a day traveling along the southern coast of the island and finally see, late in the afternoon, the first human beings they have encountered in over three months. Natives come out to greet them from the shore in outrigger canoes. At this spot they find the only passage through the reef. The Polynesians in the canoe come aboard and are followed by others. Ropes are made fast from the canoes to the raft and an effort is made to pull the Kon-Tiki ashore.

Unfortunately, an east wind is blowing and they cannot get ashore that night, and have to give up hope of making land at this time. For three more days they drift across the sea toward the Raroia and Takume reefs. They almost miss the reefs but an eat wind carries them toward them. They make preparations for the end of the voyage. Everything of value is made fast and on the morning of August 4 they run aground on the Raroia reef. As the seas come in over them they hang on for dear life. Finally, they are safe. The raft itself, however, is smashed apart. Before breaking up, the Kon-Tiki had sent a radio message to the station at Rarotonga Island, informing them of their fortunes. The voyage is over, they are alive, and they have run ashore on an uninhabited South Sea island. They drink coconut juice, stretch out on the ground, and enjoy their tropical retreat.

Comment:

Dangerous coastal currents finally snare the Kon-Tiki, but not until the journey is completed. Unable to control the direction of their raft, Heyerdahl and his fellow travelers flounder; nevertheless, they have spent three months on the sea (April 27 to August 4, 1947) and thereby have achieved one of the most remarkable feats of human ingenuity and daring, particularly noteworthy in an age seeking comfort, security, and automated luxury.

KON-TIKI

TEXTUAL ANALYSIS

CHAPTER EIGHT: AMONG POLYNESIANS

....

The little island on which the Kon-Tiki has come ashore is uninhabited. The men soon come to know every part of the island. They bring ashore various parts of the vessel which had been washed ashore, and eventually try to establish radio contact with the various stations that are interested in the whereabouts. Several days later they meet their first natives and soon they are able to travel across the lagoon separating the island from another one to the north. In their conversations with the natives it is learned that the legend of Kon-Tiki is still as strong on these islands as it is farther east. The men partake of the hospitality of the natives and enjoy the native hula dances; they treat the natives for various ailments with the medical supplies which they have been able to salvage. Each is made an honorary chief of the island by the natives.

One night they make radio contact with the island of Rarotonga; later, they receive a message from Tahiti informing them that the schooner Tamara is being sent to bring them to

Tahiti. Soon, after a sad farewell to the one hundred and twenty natives of Raroia, they are on the way to Papeete, Tahiti, where they arrive after a four-day trip. Here the author meets the chief Teriieroo, head of the seventeen native chiefs on the island. They have a great feast at his house in the Papenoo Valley and live carefree days under the sun. Days pass into weeks.

One day, the Norwegian steamer Thor I comes from Samoa to Tahiti to pick up the expedition. They leave, after throwing wreaths in the hope that they might do as Chief Teriieroo has said, "If you wish to come back to Tahiti, you must throw a wreath out into the lagoon when the boat goes."

In an appendix, Heyerdahl notes that his migration theory, as such, was not proved by the success of the Kon-Tiki. He did prove that the Pacific Islands can be reached by balsa raft from South America, something never definitively shown previously.

Comment:

The final chapter of *Kon-Tiki* is anticlimactic, since the voyage itself has been completed. Heyerdahl was able to ascertain from the voyage that: (1) Primitive people could have reached the South Seas by sailing from South America. (2) Distance itself is not the important consideration. What is important is that the wind and the ocean current have the same unchanging direction throughout the year. (3) The South American balsawood raft has properties previously unknown to science. (4) The Trade Winds (those constantly blowing toward the Equator and influenced by the rotation of the earth) and Equatorial Currents move westward in an unvarying pattern.

AKU-AKU

TEXTUAL ANALYSIS

CHAPTER ONE: DETECTIVES OFF TO THE END OF THE WORLD

....

Thor Heyerdahl, the Norwegian ethnologist, having passed Easter Island on the Kon-Tiki raft, is currently engaged in preparing an expedition to that desolate island owned by Chile, Easter Island, in the eastern Pacific.

He consults his friends, Thomas and Wilhelm, of the Fred Olsen Line, about the type of craft to be used. They decide upon a large diesel-propelled boat, rented from the Greenland fishing grounds. The passengers include his wife and family, a boy and girl, five archeologists, a doctor, a photographer, and a crew of thirteen. They have provisions for one year.

Amid hopes, fears, and doubts, and with the patronage of H.R.H. Prince Olav of Norway, and the permission of the governments of Chile, Great Britain, and France, the ship sets sail on its voyage halfway around the world. On the high prow of the ship are painted the emblems of the sacred birdmen of Easter Island.

Comment:

After his world-famous voyage aboard the raft Kon-Tiki, Heyerdahl found no difficulty in winning support for his trip to Easter Island. The governments of Norway (the book is dedicated to His Majesty King Olav V, who, as Crown Prince, was the patron of the expedition), Chile, Great Britain, and France gave their patronage to the expedition. What a difference, Heyerdahl must have thought, when he compared the living conditions aboard the trawler with those of the wooden raft! His wife had desired to accompany him on the Kon-Tiki voyage but Heyerdahl had preferred that she remain at home to care for their children. Now there is no problem - they decide to bring the boy and girl with them to share the adventures of their trip.

Easter Island (Rapa Nui) is one of the most remote and deserted places in the world. It has an area of 46 square miles and a population of 850 people. Situated in the South Pacific 2,300 miles west of the South American country of Chile (to which it belongs), Easter Island is generally believed to be of volcanic origin and is now covered with grasslands swept by the trade winds.

AKU-AKU

TEXTUAL ANALYSIS

CHAPTER TWO: WHAT AWAITED US AT THE WORLD'S NAVEL

....

After fourteen days of travel, the ship comes silently upon Easter Island. Since there are no harbors or wharves, the island can be reached only by small landing craft. Humanlike statues greet them in the night. A celebration is called for aboard ship and the author gives a lecture on the history of the island. The natives call it the "Navel of the World"" and others salute it as Rapa Nui. However, no one knows its true name. It is called Easter Island because the Dutchman Roggeveen discovered it on Easter Day, 1722.

Heyerdahl, along with other adventurers, was intrigued by the great stone figures placed all over the island. They are highly polished, perfectly carved, and fitted together without cement and mortar. Their gods were, evidently, fervently worshipped and the natives buried their dead beneath them. The natives were friendly but lived very crudely. The earlier expeditions saw very few women and children, and it was later learned that they had hid from the strangers in subterranean caves.

Comment:

The statues which Heyerdahl and the expedition see are carved from "tufa," a general name for a kind of porous stone found in the waters of certain springs. Its chief component is lime. Throughout the island these huge stones may be found. Some have hieroglyphics (hidden and symbolic writings, usually in pictures) written on them; others have been shaped from single blocks of stone into unusual stone heads. The statues range in height from ten to forty feet and some weigh over fifty tons.

Like other explorers to the island, Heyerdahl has a theory about the history and significance of the statues. This theory forms part of the interest the reader has in the earlier part of the book. Controversy has raged in recent years about the date of their origin. (See Critical Commentary.) One can easily imagine the kind of puzzling thoughts Heyerdahl had when he first saw them: What are they? For what were they used? How could past ages move such giant statues across the island? And, of course, the reader of *Aku-Aku*, at this point, is asking himself precisely the same puzzling questions.

AKU-AKU

TEXTUAL ANALYSIS

CHAPTER THREE: IN VOLCANIC GAS TUNNELS

....

Natives are hired to help excavate the lava-encrusted soil. A priest, Father Sebastian Englert, is the spiritual leader of the natives, and Heyerdahl and his party win the friendship of the natives by attending Mass. Religion plays an important part in the lives of the natives. There is evidence, according to Heyerdahl, that Easter Island was once inhabited by two races and cultures, one of whom was white and more highly esteemed than the other. With great difficulty, Heyerdahl, Father Englert, and a guide explore a subterranean cave, proceeding through slimy, dangerous tunnels.

The mayor of the island, Pedro Atan, and the governor, Captain Arnaldo Curti (of the Chilean government), greet Heyerdahl and his expedition upon their arrival. The expedition keeps their anchorage at the northern tip at Anakena, although their first anchorage was on the eastern side of the island at the village of Hotuiti.

Comment:

Father Englert is considered by many people in Chile to be the "uncrowned king" of the island. In other words, he is the single greatest force or power among the inhabitants. Clearly, Meyerdahl saw the need to become friendly with this influential priest; with him as a friend his stay on Easter Island could be made much more comfortable and profitable; with him as an enemy Heyerdahl could expect to accomplish little - if anything at all.

AKU-AKU

TEXTUAL ANALYSIS

CHAPTER FOUR: THE MYSTERY OF THE EASTER ISLAND GIANTS

....

Huge stone sculptures, some sixty-nine feet high, with long ears and unusual top-knots of red stone on their heads, abound near the volcano. All are the same in feature, though not in size. But the red stone land is seven miles away. How were these large top-knots (Pukaos) transported? Discovery of an ancient wall reveals three kinds of architecture representing what Heyerdahl believes to be the three past epochs of Easter Island's history: (1) a highly skilled culture; (2) Stone Age living; (3) war and cannibalism.

Comment:

The study of the art of primitive peoples can reveal the level of their civilization. The subjects which men choose to carve in rock indicate much of what they believe in, what they own, and what they wish to obtain. The level of the craftsmanship

in art also suggests the quality of a people's achievement. To Heyerdahl, the different kinds of expression found in the art of these statues and walls parallel stages in the history of Easter Island.

We can imagine the reaction of the natives to Heyerdahl's knowledge of the stone sculpture. They, like many simple-living people, believed him to be divinely inspired because he knew so much of their past. Naturally, many of them were anxious to sell the statues which they had to members of the expedition. Unfortunately, however, many of the pieces which they believed to be of value were actually very recently made and, therefore, were of little value to the explorers. In Heyerdahl's view, the present population of Easter Island is comprised of descendants of a victorious Polynesian invasion by which the island's natives were conquered in battle sometime in what he refers to as the third epoch.

AKU-AKU

TEXTUAL ANALYSIS

CHAPTER FIVE: THE LONG EARS' SECRET

All does not remain peaceful and quiet on this remote island. Tragically, two native children, including the mayor's daughter, drown when their launch capsizes as they are returning from a picnic. Sorrowfully, but with philosophic resignation, the mayor accepts her death: "She's well off. She's always been good. She's with the Virgin Mary."

Continuing their excavations, the group is able to resolve three "mysteries" of Easter Island: (1) It is possible to build a stone figure in a year. (2) About two hundred natives can haul a statue effectively. (3) A large top-knot of red stone could be placed in the head of a figure by the use of a ramp made from a pyramid of stones.

Heyerdahl excavates a long, deep pit, probably one used as a defense in the war between the "long ears" natives (long ear lobes) and the "short ears."

Comment:

The unfortunate deaths of the children underscore the difficulties which scientists often encounter when doing research in remote countries. Quite often it is necessary that local guides be employed to direct expeditions to favorable sites for excavations. Unless a friendly atmosphere between the natives and the "strangers" can be created and maintained, much trouble and limited progress can be expected. It is natural to expect some of the superstitious natives on Easter Island to link the misfortune of the children with the arrival of Heyerdahl's ship. Fortunately, however, because of the natives' good sense and the religious instruction they have received from Father Englert, no prolonged interruption of the research occurs.

AKU-AKU

TEXTUAL ANALYSIS

CHAPTER SIX: SUPERSTITION AGAINST SUPERSTITION

....

The island abounds in superstition and Heyerdahl must find a way to surmount it in order to gain entrance to the family caves where, he supposes, valuable art treasures lie. One night, Lazarus, the mayor's assistant, enters Heyerdahl's tent and offers him an unusual-looking sculpture. Heyerdahl learns that it is from his wife's "family" cave where there are many more "serious things." Lazarus also tells Heyerdahl where there are other ancient tablets, but he fears the Aku-Aku, or island spirits, and will not show him where the entrance is located. Heyerdahl tells the mayor and Lazarus of his dangerous travels and that his Aku-Aku has protected him; he will pray to his spirit to produce a sculptured whale from among the stones. (Lazarus had, meanwhile, planted one there.) In the process of upturning the stones, two other whale carvings are also discovered! Heyerdahl is subsequently brought many treasures from the caves of Lazarus.

High on the southwest cliffside of Orongo, wall carvings of "Totora" or reed boats are discovered and similar-looking reeds are soon found growing profusely on Easter Island. They are South American-type reeds. On the southwest of the island at Rano Rarraku, a statue is uncovered, revealing a large reed vessel with masts on it. Heyerdahl sets the Pakarati brothers to building two reed or "pora" boats, which they finish and sail on the Pacific - to the amazement of the islanders. The natives had never really seen these large reed boats in movement.

Ruins of a temple are found in Rano Kao on the southeast tip of the island. More carvings are found, depicting these reed vessels. Heyerdahl thinks the paved pathways, leading to the sea, must have been used for unloading these ships. Lazarus brings wood and sculptured pieces depicting these ships from his family's cave.

The mayor, having professed to own a few caves, now promises to bring Heyerdahl there - if he receives gifts from the expedition.

Comment:

In this chapter, Heyerdahl's ingenuity and resourcefulness are demonstrated in the manner in which he wins the confidence and consent of the mayor of Easter Island. The Aku-Aku, which he used to win permission to examine Lazarus' cave, was one of a kind of statue used by "sensible" natives to warn off evil spirits and otherwise perform for the benefit of its owner.

The discovery of the "Totora" reed boat carvings on the cliffside of Orongo leads Heyerdahl to think that he has

discovered further evidence to link the early history of Easter Island with that of Peru, inasmuch as such reeds are native to the South American countryside. Tied together into bundles and made into rafts, they are buoyant and sturdy. It is possible that reed ships have been built by early Peruvians to cross the Pacific to Easter Island.

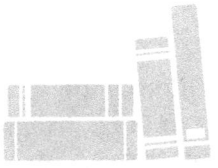

AKU-AKU

TEXTUAL ANALYSIS

CHAPTER SEVEN: MEETING THE CAVES' DUMB GUARDIANS

The Pinto, a warship from Chile, arrives at Easter Island. After becoming intoxicated, the mayor brags to the Chilean scientist, Professor Pena, about the worth of the stone sculptures in the caves on the island. Heyerdahl lessens the professor's displeasure by telling of his earlier agreement to send all the sculptures to Chile when he has finished his research. The mayor asserts that his cave is as old as the original "Long Ear" natives. In vain, Heyerdahl attempts to persuade the mayor to show him the cave. After the ship leaves, a mild epidemic of "concongo" or influenza spreads throughout the island. Heyerdahl nearly succeeds in persuading a native, Estevan, and his wife into permitting him to visit their family cave, but once again, he is unsuccessful.

> Comment:

One can understand why the members of the Chilean expedition, who had legal rights to recover any sculptures found on the island, would be indignant after assuming that Heyerdahl would return to Norway with the work he had excavated. Heyerdahl's explanation eliminates the friction which the mayor's disclosure began. He agrees to surrender all of the treasures he finds to Chile once he has finished with his scientific research.

Heyerdahl has great difficulty trying to convince either the mayor or Estevan to let him visit their secret family caves. The superstition of the natives may have prevented them from giving Heyerdahl access to the caves, but one wonders if Heyerdahl was not somewhat skeptical about the reality of the caves. He is forced to do favors to the mayor and others, hoping that one day he may be able to visit one of the caves.

AKU-AKU

TEXTUAL ANALYSIS

CHAPTER EIGHT: INTO THE SECRET CAVES

....

Atan, the youngest of the mayor's brothers, receives permission from him to show Heyerdahl his (Atan's) cave. After a ceremony to the Aku-Aku gods, a descent is made into an ominous black hole. Heyerdahl is first greeted by two grinning white skulls. Also in the cave, however, are many invaluable art treasures, each a new ethnographic find. Later, another native, Lazarus, invites Heyerdahl to his cave, called "Cliff of the Tropical Bird." After a treacherous descent down a steep lava cliff, Heyerdahl enters the cave. He discovers many valuable stone sculptures in this gloomy chamber.

At last, success. Heyerdahl finally visits two of the ancient caves on Easter Island. These caves may be compared to family burial tombs in which the bones of each generation are stored to protect them from being unearthed by enemies. In each cave are extremely old and unusual sculptures of men and animals. Heyerdahl removes only the most interesting of the objects from the caves.

Comment:

The commonly held belief that the statues of Easter Island were the "product of local imagination" was, according to Heyerdahl, based on inadequate information. Some specimens of statues displayed similarities to the art of other Pacific islands, suggesting that they may be the product of immigrant natives of earlier epochs.

AKU-AKU

TEXTUAL ANALYSIS

CHAPTER NINE: AMONG GODS AND DEVILS

....

The mayor of Easter Island is suddenly stricken with the "concongo" epidemic. While his fever is high, he promises to permit Heyerdahl (or "Kon-Tiki," as the natives call him) to visit his family cave. The mayor, Estevan, and Atan, the mayor's brother, try to deceive Heyerdahl by misrepresenting the authenticity of certain sculptures. The natives, upon hearing of this deception, become angry. Santiago Pakarati, a native, working for the expedition, offers to accompany Heyerdahl to a cave in which ten sculptures are found.

Atan, the mayor's brother, reveals that his brother-in-law, Andres Haoa, has a cave. But Andres, although he is willing to reveal it, is opposed by his younger brother Juan, a very religious and superstitious man. Heyerdahl, however, by pretending that his Aku-Aku has magical powers, persuades Juan to bring them into the cave. Rare earthenware jars are discovered inside. Juan, however, makes Heyerdahl promise not to take any more sculptures from the natives. Therefore, when a couple bring him seventeen stone sculptures from a cave called "Eye of the Straw Image," Heyerdahl explains that all of them must be returned to the cave on the day of his departure. Once more the mayor attempts to deceive Heyerdahl, bringing him to a false cave and not his ancestors' "Ororoina" cave. Juan, the mayor's son, however, does direct him to a cave which yields twenty-six valuable sculptures. Their research work finished, Heyerdahl and his expedition depart from Easter Island.

Comment:

This chapter reveals the contrast between good and evil among the Easter Island natives. The title of the chapter, "Among Gods and Devils," may apply not merely to the sculptures found in the caves but to the different kinds of men that Heyerdahl was forced to deal with on the island. Twice, we are told, the mayor attempts to deceive him regarding the sculptures and the caves. Yet Santiago, Andres, and Juan Haoa, and even the mayor's son, do show Heyerdahl the treasures of their secret caves.

Many previously unexplored caves were not examined. The contents of the caves were, chiefly, small stone sculptures, but paper manuscripts, pots, wood carvings, and other goods were also found. Although it was impossible to date the sculptures, Heyerdahl estimated that they were created before the birth of Christ. The natives' habit of living in caves was probably a result of their need for safety from every attack made during the island's civil wars.

AKU-AKU

TEXTUAL ANALYSIS

CHAPTER TEN: A RUINED CITY IN THE CLOUDS

....

The next stop is Pitcairn Island, the locale of the novel *Mutiny on the Bounty*. It does a thriving business selling wood carvings of flying fish and models of the ship Bounty. After a stop at Mangariva, a French island, the expedition reaches Rapa Ita, where, since 1791, no archeological exploration has taken place. Heyerdahl, after considerable difficulty, finds workers to dig excavations on one of the island's twelve hilltops. Each of the hilltops, it is discovered, is a link in a complex fortification in which earlier natives had lived. They are 160 feet high and extend for 1,300 feet.

It is learned that the kings of the island had a secret burial place, the "Cave of the Kings" in the Anarua Valley - tombs which have never been discovered.

Comment:

Pitcairn Island, celebrated in the famous sea novel, *Mutiny on the Bounty*, by Nordhoff and Hall, actually contains little for scientists interested in archeological exploration. It is surprising to find commercial trinkets and mementos being sold in this remote Pacific island.

The excavation that Heyerdahl's diggers explored on Rapa Ita is known as Morongo Uta. Grouped together, the fortifications on the island are considered the largest in Polynesia.

The island of Papa Hi (little papa) was discovered by Captain Vancouver in 1791. He had seen the island's strange castlelike hilltops but did not explore them. The population of Papa Hi is 2,789, and of this number traditionally more women work than men.

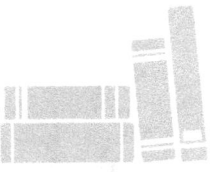

AKU-AKU

TEXTUAL ANALYSIS

CHAPTER ELEVEN: MY AKU-AKU SAYS

....

While swimming in a mountain cave of Nuka-Hiva's Taipi Valley, Heyerdahl begins an imaginary conversation with his Aku-Aku. They discuss Heyerdahl's theory that centuries ago natives from Peru may have crossed the Pacific Ocean and settled in the Easter Islands. The Peruvians, like the early natives of Easter Island, used to lengthen their ear lobes so that they hung down to their shoulders. The Aku-Aku asks, "Where did these short ears come from?" Heyerdahl replies that they arrived from other islands in Polynesia.

A few hours later, Heyerdahl is aboard the expedition ship. Following a local custom, each of the passengers throws the wreath of flowers that had been around his neck into the water as the ship departs.

Comment:

In his last chapter Heyerdahl uses a clever technique, an imaginary conversation between himself and his Aku-Aku, thereby giving himself an opportunity to summarize his theories about the early history of Easter Island. The Aku-Aku asks the questions and Heyerdahl gives the answers. Heyerdahl's sense of humor is keen; in one instance, after a lengthy explanation by Heyerdahl, the Aku-Aku falls asleep!

Plaster casts of the statues (some eight feet high) were made to be sent to the Kon-Tiki Museum in Oslo, Norway. Heyerdahl has completed another adventurous and scientifically rewarding expedition in the ancient islands of the Pacific Ocean.

CRITICAL COMMENTARY

There has been much discussion of Heyerdahl's theories: Waldemar Kaempffert, writing in the *New York Times* (August 17, 1947), found similarities between Heyerdahl's theories and those of Professor G. N. Lewis of the University of California, and A. Posnansky. The majority of anthropologists disagree with Heyerdahl's theories, believing the Polynesians to be descendants of Asiatic and not South American tribes. But what matters, as Kaempffert has pointed out, is that Heyerdahl "proved by his epic voyage that it is possible to reach Polynesia from Peru on a Polynesian raft."

But what about the theories resulting from the Easter Island voyage? Heyerdahl maintains:

1. Easter Island was probably settled by South Americans, not Asians. If Easter Island were discovered by Asians then it must have been the last one discovered, because of its remote distance from Asia. It would, therefore, have the shortest period of civilization. Heyerdahl says, "If, on the other hand, the seafarers came from South America, then Easter Island would be the nearest, the first reached, and possessing the oldest culture in all Polynesia."

2. Perhaps Heyerdahl's "principal" discovery was that the ancestors of the present natives on Easter Island probably arrived there relatively late in history. Heyerdahl maintains that the culture of Easter Island was not a "coherent" one, of a "brief explosive bloom," but a "restless exchange" of three "predeveloped" cultural systems which led, finally, to decadence and dissolution.

3. Easter Island is alone among the islands of the Pacific which demonstrate the "highly specialized masonry technique" otherwise characteristic of Peru, South America. Excavations by Heyerdahl's group showed that this masonry was characteristic of the first settlers on Easter Island and not the two following cultural epochs.

4. Statues of Easter Island also resembled those of ancient Peru. Two statues in particular showed more resemblance to specialized "pre-Inca" statues in Tiahuanaco (Peru) than to any other statues in the Pacific Islands.

5. Statues made by craftsmen of other islands in the Marquesas group, e.g., Hiva Oa and Nuku Hiva, were probably made centuries after those found on Easter Island. By using carbon samples taken from material underneath the platforms of the Marquesas group, Heyerdahl asserts that their comparatively late origin (A.D. 1300-1500) explains why it is unlikely that they are prototypes (original models) for the Easter Island group.

6. Native tradition on Easter Island insists that man-made fortifications were made by earlier generations. Certain scientific opinion disregards the people's belief, however, maintaining that the excavations are merely natural formations - depressions in the land. Heyerdahl says that these depressions have been "skillfully transformed" by man into "elaborate defense positions."

7. By tracing the family lives of the present natives of Easter Island, Heyerdahl asserts that all can be traced to "long-ear" natives who survived the island's civil war. Also, by conducting a series of experiments with the natives, he maintained that it is possible to carve, transport, and build large stone statues similar to those on Easter Island by utilizing native help and equipment.

8. Botanists (scientists who study plants) have demonstrated that Peruvian crops have been transported to some of the Polynesian islands by early voyagers. Easter Island agriculture was based extensively on the growth of a Kumura or Peruvian potato even before the first European explorers landed. Another Peruvian product in wide use was the Totora reed, a plant used to make wooden mats, baskets, and certain kinds of masts for ships.

9. Discoveries made in Orongo and Vinapu revealed that the early settlers of the first epoch had, like the Peruvian Indians, a reverence for the sun.

10. Blood samples taken from the natives of Easter Island and sent to Melbourne, Australia, for examinations showed that there are remarkable blood conformities between the original inhabitants of North and South America and the Easter Islanders. Moreover, the contrast with Asiatic blood characteristics - those found in Indonesians, Malaysians, and others is very pronounced.

11. Several previously "secret" caves for living, storage, or hiding were examined on Easter Island. The chief items discovered in these caves were stone sculptures, wood carvings, pots, paper manuscripts, and other goods were occasionally found also. Although it was impossible to date the contents of the caves, Heyerdahl believes that they antedated Christianity.

ESSAY QUESTIONS AND ANSWERS

....

Question: In what ways do books such as *Kon-Tiki* and *Aku-Aku* differ from a novel as a literary work?

Answer:

1. Primarily, of course, both of Heyerdahl's books are true accounts of his experiences. In a novel we may find **realism** or historical background employed, i.e., names of real cities, people, and events, but the essential framing of incidents and dialogue is based on imaginative, not actual, experience.

2. Both books are chiefly travel books. Heyerdahl is less concerned with deep exploration of character or motive, as a novelist usually is, than with relating the adventurous aspects of his journeys and setting forth his ethnological theories briefly and clearly so that the general reader can understand the major import of his ideas.

3. Heyerdahl cannot employ such devices as symbolism to express his general views. Quite often a modern writer will use objects, characters, colors, and other

things to suggest meaning: for example, a dark, hooded character may represent death. In reading a novel, a person often finds many such symbols which add to the total effect the writer is wishing to produce.

Question: What was the purpose of the Kon-Tiki voyage?

Answer: Heyerdahl had become fascinated with similarities existing between the art of the Marquesas Islands of the Pacific Ocean and that of the Indians of Peru. The Poe-Inca Indians had worshipped the sun god "Kon," and the leader of the Indians "Kon-Tiki," the man who represented the sun god on earth (who had fled with some followers from his enemies - the Indians from the Andes Mountains - about five hundred years after the birth of Christ).

The principal aim of the Kon-Tiki voyage was to prove that Peruvians could have crossed the Pacific Ocean in balsa-wood rafts using the power of strong ocean currents.

Question: What did the voyage of the Kon-Tiki prove?

Answer:

1. Simply, that it is possible to cross the ocean on wooden rafts; this feat opened up a great deal of speculation and further research concerning possible origins of the natives in the Marquesas Group.

2. Equatorial currents and the trade winds (which blow towards the Equator and are influenced by the earth's rotation) move westward in an unvarying pattern.

3. The wind and the ocean current have the same unchanging direction throughout the year. This is the important consideration in judging whether an ocean voyage was possible centuries ago - not merely, for example, the distance between Peru and the Marquesas.

4. The South American balsa tree has outstanding properties formerly unknown.

Question: What were the chief results of Heyerdahl's expedition to Easter Island?

Answer: The voyage to Easter Island was prompted by Heyerdahl's curiosity about the statues and other objects which he had learned resembled South American art. By excavating at Easter Island and other islands of the Marquesas group he was able to arrive at certain theories concerning the history of the Polynesian people. Of primary importance are his arguments that there are numerous similarities between the Polynesians and the South American Peruvian Indians. The reasons Heyerdahl gives lend support to his theory that the early immigrants to Polynesia may have been from Peru. (See Critical Commentary for fuller treatment of this question.)

Question: Describe Heyerdahl's writing style.

Answer: Style in a writer is like a fingerprint in a man. It's there; it's unique and the person can be identified by it. In writing, of course, a person must usually be able to write clearly, logically, and simply in putting words together if he is to approach what is loosely termed "style." Heyerdahl's writing discloses several general characteristics. Rather than give a curt, blanket-like estimate of his writing, let us examine certain major characteristics:

1. He is direct in statement. Fortunately for the reader, Heyerdahl has an incisive, attentive mind which seeks maximum explanation with minimum of digression.

2. His language is colorful. Heyerdahl uses concrete appeals to the senses throughout the book. Unlike many writers, he avoids vague, general terms, giving us the picture or the touch: "When we got through this dense barricade which skirted the edge of the overgrown lake, the whole crater marsh spread out before us like a patch-work quilt of brown, yellow, green, blue and black." (*Aku-Aku*, p. 187)

3. He knows how to tell a story. A good writer attempts in his opening lines to win the interest of the reader. After whetting his curiosity, the writer must continually inform, surprise, delight, or otherwise sustain the reader's interest in the work. That Heyerdahl is a born storyteller can be measured by the overwhelming response of the public to his books. By taking just two examples, the opening lines of both books, we can see how Heyerdahl's gift for getting the reader's attention by appealing to his curiosity has been used:

Kon-tiki: "Once in a while you find yourself in an odd situation."

Aku-Aku: "I had no Aku-Aku. Nor did I know what an Aku-Aku was..."

4. His humor is natural, warm, and consistent. There is a playful sense of fun and an ability to laugh at his own misjudgment and mistakes in Heyerdahl's writing. Such humor is part of the man's total view of the world and himself. His attitude toward the turtles, whales, sharks, dolphins, and other fish the Kon-Tiki meets invests the creatures with life-like personalities and adds greatly to the enjoyment of the voyage. In *Aku-Aku* his portrayal of the natives' unusual ways and his imaginary conversation with his Aku-Aku in the final chapter are written with light, engaging touches.

BIBLIOGRAPHY

KON-TIKI

"Our Four Months on the Raft," *Reader's Digest*, November, 1947.

"Cruise of the Kon-Tiki," *Life Magazine*, October 20, 1947.

"Westward Voyage," *Time Magazine*, April 21, 1947.

"Ethnology Afloat," *Newsweek Magazine*, May 12, 1947.

"From Raft to Reef," *Newsweek Magazine*, August 25, 1947.

See also *Current Biography*, December, 1947.

AKU-AKU

Those wishing to learn more about Heyerdahl's theories concerning the origins of the Polynesians should consult: Heyerdahl, Thor. *American Indians in the Pacific*.

RECENT SEA EXPLORATION

Cousteau, Jacques-Yves. "At Home in the Sea," *National Geographic Magazine*, April, 1964.

Johnson, Irving and Electra. "New Guinea to Bali in Yankee," *National Geographic Magazine*, December, 1959.

Link, Edward. "Our Man in Sea Project," *National Geographic Magazine*, May, 1963.

____. "Tomorrow on the Deep Frontier," *National Geographic Magazine*, June, 1964.

____. "Outpost under the Ocean," *National Geographic Magazine*, April, 1965.

www.ingramcontent.com/pod-product-compliance
Lightning Source LLC
LaVergne TN
LVHW021736060526
838200LV00052B/3303